A
HEART
Searching for Its
SOUL

CARL FAZIO

Some names have been changed to respect the privacy of people mentioned in this book.

Printed in the United States of America

Published in Hellertown, PA

ISBN 978-1-958711-19-4

Library of Congress Control Number available upon request

2 4 6 8 10 9 7 5 3 1

Cover design by Leanne Coppola

For information or to purchase bulk copies, contact Jennifer@BrightCommunications.net.

To my wife, Christine

I met my wife, Christine, in a night club in June of 1973. It was a warm comfortable summer night, and all the stars were in their designated positions, sparkling in the evening sky. Whatever celestial influences decided our fate, we knew we'd be together for the rest of our lives. Our introductory conversation was initially comedic and casual. Little did I know that she would become the most valuable person in my (at that time) uncertain life. By February 24, 1974, in the witness of family and friends, we were married in Saint Aloysins Church in Wilkes-Barre, Pennsylvania. Our wedding song was "We've Only Just Begun."

During the past 47 years of marriage, she has been everything a wife could possibly be, and more.

When we first met, some of her acquaintances warned her that I was a "womanizer, and she would be better off without me!" Her response was, "I make my own judgments." She may well have been better off without me, and perhaps enjoy a better quality of life, with some other man and going in another direction. But I would not! Christine has been the ultimate paradigm of fidelity and love for all in her family. She is the best example of integrity I have ever known. My life without her would've been an endless drift of emptiness, as it was before I met her.

She was and still is blonde, tall, slender, and gorgeous, with a cosmopolitan air of sophistication. Our first kiss under a soft lit lamppost was impossible to describe. I loved her instantly and will continue loving her into the beyond.

Whatever transcendent forces arranged our unity made me one of the luckiest men on this planet. Her instincts and wisdom have been a proven value for all throughout her professional career. As we have aged and grown in our united wisdom, the original vows of "Until death do we part" now have a more impactful meaning, as a philosophic extension of those marital vows we now have a metaphysical one, a spiritual commitment as we cross over to reside together forever.

He was in search of an elusive soul.
His life is an unextinguishable fire.
A song he couldn't sing to a special face that glows.
Angry, frustrated, he becomes a liar.

A heart in search of its mysterious soul,
Clung to secret lies, changing them into truths.
And lived a life of theater and show.
For a search that only ends without proof.

A sage took the stage and said,
"You're a corpus being born on a warm day in the fall.
That soul you're looking for isn't your concrete head.
It's your conscious state that carries the social ball."

Contents

If Lies

You can't remember what you never learned.

You can't forget what you never knew.

Are you then entitled to the Democracy you haven't earned?

Or the fruits of Washington's soldiers who fought for you?

When you walk into a precinct to cast a vote on election day,

Ask someone who wore the uniform of the fighting men, who knew

The blood-soaked sands of true patriots, who on battlefields lay,

So, you will remember the cost of freedom paid—for you.

It's 2022, a time in our USA when lies rule the day.

Arrows are in their quivers, and the medieval bows are strung.

They, the liars, do remember, but in an untruthful way.

Recruit those who never knew and believe the BS being slung.

You can't remember what you never learned.
You can't forget what you never knew.
If the lies destroy the truth and turn into facts,
Your freedom of which you never learned
May never come back.

The Pond

People were all dressed in their winter attire, gathered around the town's skating pond.

Some were showing off their twists, jumps, and turns to demonstrate they still were strong.

An older gentleman, who never missed these winter events, sat there excited with his dimming eyes.

As observing adults teach children the basics on ice, his withering, old heart swelled with pride.

With a little shiver, he rubbed his cold hands together and rolled up his wool-lined jacket collar.

There was some music playing as the skaters were coupling off, mostly young mothers and fathers, who would hear the DJ, "Couples only," holler.

Tearfully, he remembered his younger years when he and Patty were the skaters' paradigm.

And so he slowly drifted off with his scarf covering his face and ears into a cozy nostalgic dream.

In his dream, he and his young sweetheart danced all around the icy pond, stopping for an occasional kiss.

Her name was Patricia, more commonly known by all others as Patty, and she was all his.

They waltzed arm in arm, enjoying it with a passion so intense no others could match.

They weren't alone in their talent. There was a Mary and her partner, Joe Shorty Latch.

His dream ended as he awoke with a smile on his wrinkled brow and fresh snow on his grey mustache.

Often the couples would clear the ice for the cheering crowd.

Never bragging about their talent, but they were socially proud.

The late day light was giving way to December's darkening, darkest sky.

A larger crowd of evening watchers gathered, and younger skaters with their new skate laces proved hard to tie.

As teenagers were piling more logs onto the bonfire,

The sky around the local pond was a crimson, romantic red.

The old man, wanting to find a seat closer to the raging fire, shifting his weight was almost frantic.

While observing his difficulty, a strong, young man who was passing by gave him a helping hand.

Without any difficulty, he soon found a park bench where no one was sitting, thanks to the young man.

The raging fire warmed one side of his face and body. He was at peace and fond of his pond memories.

His thoughts were broken when a pretty, young girl skated up and gave him a cup of chocolate, steaming hot!

Thankful to God for the full life he was able to live and now for the pretty, young girl's generous thought.

Music, laughter, and sounds made everything right for the town's pond on a skater's December night.

And there he sat, bundled and blessed, so grateful for the magic of another beautiful pond sight.

Suddenly, he wiped the steam from his glasses, in disbelief of what he might be seeing.

Focusing as best that he could with his aging eyes, he felt certain it was her, a real living being.

In his unsteady gait, he cautiously avoided her seeing him approach, as an old man whose walking wasn't too sturdy.

"Well, I'll be damned, Mary, is that you? Is there any room under that lap blanket for two?"

"Saddle up, there's plenty of room, don't you worry!"

Time flew by as Mary and her old friend John got caught up on the past forty years.

They laughed at the timely similarities and often sad events of their passing spouses, often unable to suppress their tears.

Mary and Patty were ice skating rivals, both beautiful to watch and often changing partners on the pond.

Mary looked long and hard at John, ending the moment said, "It's been much too long, John, oh so long."

"Mary, let's do this again, maybe tomorrow? You pretend you're still a young girl, and I'm still that bad boy."

The evening was just getting started, and more families were joining the crowds, seeking the same old joy.

Mary sadly said, "I have to get back and feed the cat, then call my sister-in-law and try telling her about seeing you at the pond. I just know she'll be full of the hows and whys."

The flames were burning higher, and the sparks were like winter fireflies, showing off their magic in the dark, winter sky.

It was past John's bedtime as he walked away from the ice skaters, who were just beginning to build their own memories.

He was happy, happier he thought than any man of his age had a right to be.

Tomorrow, he'd see Mary again; they'd have fun.

Well, nothing could ever replace Patty, the thought wasn't a bit funny.

He and Mary could laugh and do things, maybe spend some of their security money.

It wasn't a matter of an old, wrinkle-faced man falling in love one more time. Love is forever, without an expiration date.

The whole thing happens; it's a thing called fate!

Mary, excited about meeting John at the skater's pond, ran to the phone and told her sister-in-law all about it, blanket and all.

She awoke early and searched the closet for her best possible clothes to wear; nothing fit. She was no longer a small.

She called John at the number he gave her yesterday. It rang and rang.

Maybe it was a wrong number, but for what reason?

Mary's feelings of happiness slowly faded into the throes of a lonely depression.

Again, she tried the number, and it continued to ring and ring; could this be another broken-heart lesson?

Later that day, the morning paper arrived.

Mary rushed to the obituary page.

Mary leaned against the wall and slowly slid to the floor.

She was afraid to read anymore.

She didn't move; she just stayed for the longest while.

A neighbor picked up the paper and went on to read: John Evans, 88, died peacefully in his sleep, holding a photo of Pat as a child.

His face had the most peaceful smile.

The front page of the newspaper featured a large photograph of the night scene bonfire and its flying ember.

Mary, John, Patricia, et al were the bright sparks that lit the evening sky for a little while, which then went dark forever, because there's no one left to remember.

C'est La Vie

There once sat by the sea an artist whose passion exceeds the raging seas.

Upon his easel sat an empty canvas, waiting patiently for his brush.

This would be the moment; his passion for greatness was finally here.

He would paint the ocean's glory and all its power without fear.

But the sky darkened, and raindrops reached his fresh paint, and it smeared.

As it began to appear, this may have been his best work of the year!

There was a singer, who sang love songs for all the world's lovers to hear.

Accompanied by a chorus of angels, echoing God's music from above.

Videos and radios played his music for the beating hearts passionately in love.

Yet in his own soul are the lyrics he missed, which couldn't ever be replaced.

Or ever sing of his real hidden desire, the image of his father's face.

There was this dancer, whose devotional need was to choreograph motion.

And create human movement upon the dance floor, fluid like the ocean.

She danced and danced for hours, until her passion did finally subside.

Her aching muscles signaled to her it was only the satisfaction of having tried.

Unable to produce the unique greatness of dance, what was it she was trying to hide?

There was this poet whose rhythmic soul searched for words to explain

Man's passion of all the whys, the why of all that's poignant and beautiful leads to pain.

As he ponders all the reasons why, there comes this heightened feeling of love.

He finally accepts that the answers that man seeks come only from above.

In the twin dynamics of all emotion seen between ecstasy and tragedy,

Is the dark ocean of tears in between.

There was a dim lit sidewalk café along the nocturnal Champs-Elysees.

Where artists, singers, dancers, and poets gathered at the end of their days.

Quietly they sit, sipping their wine, thinking of their passion to create something — their strife.

When they paint, sing, dance, and write, attempting to solve the mysteries of life.

Gradually, the Parisian sky darkens, and sobriety falls upon their quiet essence.

All their three-dimensional bodies fade into peaceful, poetic silhouettes.

As the Parisian night lights soften the daunting souls of the tortured passionate.

The red glow and smoke from their cigarettes are the only remains of a failed days start.

Maybe tomorrow, maybe tomorrow, on the sidewalk cafés of the Champs-Elysees,

They'll regain their tortured passions, who knows, perhaps, *plus tard*?

One Heart

Waking from a turbulent dream, he was enraged.

Unable to control the residual feelings, he set an imaginary stage.

An untenable thought pervades throughout his whole being.

Why the lingering rage? Whatever does it mean?

Raging on, no balance of a tortured mind was he able to find.

And the whys were unending; they just kept coming and coming.

To what could he ever compare? What would settle his mind?

In the mirror, he feared to stare at his tired, old, vacant eyes.

Yet, still he believed there was a truth to be realized.

He would need to send his soul on a special mission,

To a place where a dark rage matched his own dark vision.

Wherein the dark waters of the North Atlantic ocean tides.

Are angry waves smashing ships against a wharf's evil cries.

"I am dark, ugly, and mad; everything I am not makes me sad.

When I am not enraged and hating, I am manically loving."

Not softened by the tender thought of being in so many loves,

From the mirror he turns, with outstretched arms looking above.

How, dear God, how can I love so many equally apart?

Why, dear God, have you given me only one heart?

Why is that a single heart in a body can love so many things?

With a soul incapable of containing the peace of a kingdom?

Tonight, maybe I'll dream again, this time of tranquility

In the peaceful waters of a Hawaiian sea.

If and when the anger and rage subside, he'll hear the tanager sing.

To wake to a new day, sans hate or rage, longing once again to be me!

Turning the Page

In our youth, forever is time that never ends.

When older, forever is as near as tomorrow,

Just around the bend.

Black and white movies become your nocturnal friend.

If you're lucky, your journey will be free of sorrow.

Find the brightest star in an October sky.

Warm your tender heart and soul as precious time passes you by.

And quell temptations for rage

As you turn each page.

Oh, By the Way

It was just the other day when a Republican from Mississippi passed this way.

It just so happens that a hungry man asked him for a helping hand.

And this is what he had to say to the hungry man,

"Pull yourself up by the bootstraps, and you'll enjoy the fruits of this great land!"

A curious bystander, gave this reply,

"It's always easy for you guys to give him the boot."

But where and when will you provide that proverbial strap he needs to get by?"

The crowd, which slowly gathered were cheering, as one played a flute.

The Republican from Mississippi answered no questions and stoically said goodbye.

The crowd surrounded the curious bystander and gave him a salute.

As the girl was playing "God Bless America" on her instrument.

Tears ran free. It was a poignant moment.

The curious bystander, as he was leaving, tears visible in his eye.

Embarrassed by the praise said, "I'll leave it to all of you to answer the why."

Pity Me

So, there I stood in the rain, hoping for inspiration to enjoy the day.

An indolent man with nothing special to say.

I fought off the mundane urge to say what's common to say, or even to tell a lie.

To complain, "Where's the sun day after day," no fun trying just to stay dry.

Then the voice of angels, sans sight, sans the pure joy of seeing an image.

A voice echoing to all of God's creation the passion to love and be average,

"I am the God who has given you the senses to see, hear, and walk, all of your inspiration.

I am the God who shared his green trees, scent of flowers, and placid lakes. That's your inspiration?"

That song fed my soul with love of what mankind isn't but should be his fate!

So, I cried, cried for the rain and asked if my heart could begin again.

But the tears didn't stop sensing that it could be too late.

Shocked by my third eye experience, I vowed to never again complain.

Relax, Old Man

He was all set to go; his lungs were filled to capacity.

Upon a new road, his rich, red blood is charged with fresh audacity.

Idling in place, waiting for the gunshot to start the race.

To higher heights, where every heart and mind finds a better place.

Slinking and snaking around in his cranium lurks a new project.

Wherein maybe, just maybe, he'll develop a stronger rocket.

Let me see now, to continue on with this cryptic metaphor,

I'll cut off the rusty hinges on that old subliminal vault door

And peek inside to see what nuances are waiting to emerge.

And wow! Nothing is there, nothing he hasn't seen before.

Like in an old, dusty room, all that useless rust must be purged.

Well, anyway, he tried. Now it's time to deflate and exhale.

Being all set to go is nothing new for a dreamer's unlit torch.

Who spends hours on a broken swing on his broken-down porch.

Maybe tomorrow, there'll be a fresh inspiration to hit the trail.

Satisfied, with his alibi's being justified.

Tomorrow, he really must find someone to bring him his mail.

Walls Crumble and Fall

Go ahead, Mr. President, build a wall. Build it quickly and make it tall.

Make it impossible for asylum seekers et al

To scale over or underneath crawl.

From our mountains to our prairies, in the song I recall,

God blessed America, for one and for all.

Go ahead, Mr. President, take children and crying babies from their mothers' hands.

In the name of border safety and national security, you piously think some may understand.

In the pursuit of liberty and freedom, our founding fathers, they took a stand.

Documents we call a Constitution and Bill of Rights set the stage for a free people with the rule of law.

So, go ahead, Mr. President, build your wall and build it tall.

As in Berlin, a wall built by evil designed to keep freedom out did eventually fall.

As your fantasy goes up brick by brick with every evil stone, when you face God, you'll be alone.

You'll join the evil crucifiers, whose swords pierced Jesus' muscle and bone.

Your incessant lies will never part any waters or rescue a people from make believe harm's way.

Honest hard-working people will line the streets to witness you and your sycophants in disgrace one day.

The world you live in is a shield made of Bubble Wrap designed by a daddy who was full of crap.

If all is as is told, heaven is soft clouds peacefully floating with good people on long naps.

Upon entering, you surrender all your gold.

But there is a place called hell, where people like you watch your flesh blister off as you beg for forgiveness, scream and yell.

So go ahead, you miserable toad, build it and build it fast.

Like you, it will never last.

Everyone's a Star

Did you know, every star that glows
In the darkest of nights gives the brightest light.
And Alpha Centauri is a flame
Calling someone's name.

Here we are, enchanted
And firmly planted,
Awed by the mystery of a bright starry night's glow,
Unwise of what's in front of our eyes and under our
nose.

Above and beyond the billions and trillions of stars,
Transcending our human minds, you will find.
Burning stars, scouting space while burning out
For a place to spread their particles about.

Gathering together again to form a new brighter star to
emerge as family!
Each particle becomes solo stars, entering into a
constellation to become a family tree.
Of every star you see in the galaxy at night, one is your
own true light.

Your own angel watching over you, making sure you're alright.

On Earth, the way things are, only celebrities are stellar,

But in the heavens, everyone there is a star!

Did you know, of all the universal stars glowing, seven are Fazios!

While wishing upon the majestic magic of every star and white-winged angel's glow, may they enter every heart and be their own star's brightest glow.

Forward Back

I'm a forward-moving coyote, never looking back.

The past was never a matter of concern,

Until I was warned not to burn the bridge I passed,

A lesson I'm glad to have learned.

There's an image consuming me in this moment,

A building with three stories and walls of ivy,

Within the floors where a soul that was dormant

Is where this coyote discovered a place to serve society.

In a complex of 1,200 farming acres,

Two large alms houses were erected for the poor.

Wherein the residents were also their own caretakers.

A place where the homeless, sick, and hungry were once lured.

To Laurytown, where for miles the buildings could be seen.

And today it's nothing but an empty field of green.

An above-ground tunnel constructed of native wood

Became the bridge separating the women from the men.

I journeyed between them, providing care the best I could,

Never fretting or looking back, but that was then.

A time when all that mattered was the one in the den.

Time, as it inevitably must, changes everything.

The most glorious of men and beautiful flowers

Give space for the wonderful new life born each spring.

I was a forward-looking coyote, never thinking of the days or hours.

My heart was on fire, a man in a mad rush to find love.

Looking everywhere, maybe it was here, or there, or above.

Never looking to where I've been, just where I was going.

And unnoticed were the many years passing me by,

Walking by the lilies and roses, not thinking or knowing.

Now this forward-moving coyote wants to cry.

I know forward moving ultimately leads you back.

A coyote so strong, confident, and staying on track.

A tunnel between two buildings where my soul was found,

The time and place where my self-worth was born,

On 1200 acres of farmland, today is vacant grounds.

And, so the value of memory is what the coyote learned.

True, it is so that nothing ever remains the same.

A coyote crossing many bridges, and not one did he burn.

Or covet money, well, maybe just a little fame.

Now this melancholy, old coyote almost never leaves his den.

Satisfied, shuts down any thoughts of what could've been.

Long gone are the buildings and occupants whose end of lives

Ended their last chapter and the mysterious scene.

Nothing today is there of those husbands or wives.

Long forgotten are those once viable hearts and souls.

Nothing of their once presence on this Earth remains.

Sadly, where it all went no one really knows.

Time, as it does, for all ended their suffering and pain.

Gently, this gray-haired coyote covered his sad eyes.

Alone in his den, fell asleep, and quietly did die.

As outside, young coyotes howled at a moonlit sky.

Under the Snow

What's under the winter's white snow
Are all the memories of last summer's flowers
And the cut green grass under the sun's glow.

When the snow has all melted and gone away,
Will a new summer bring grass just as green?
Will the flowers and trees bloom the same way?
Will I walk normal, or is it just a dream?

What mystery lies under the winter snow
When the days are longer, and time reveals
The truth of what wasn't seen from my window.

When the tanager is back in his evergreen tree,
The grass, flowers, and trees will be everything.
It's the beauty of them all together that makes me be
me!

What lies beneath the blanketed winter snow
Are thawed hearts, hoping for a new beginning
With greener grass, brighter flowers, and prettier birds
To love and be loved while riding on their wings.

My dog barks for something to eat; the cat's eyes glow
The February night is shutting down the light.
The melting snow stops. I move from the window
And walk when my quads aren't so tight.

A Window View

Out of the deep, virgin, white fallen snow

Stands a large oak, which took 30 years to grow.

And still has brown leaves that never fell last fall.

As an observer, I muse, *How did it grow so tall?*

Basking in the summer's sun, sprouting leaves in every branch,

Undaunted by the maple tree who's in a proud stance,

Never reached my height and doesn't produce any fruit,

I drop acorns on the ground every fall near my roots.

My fruit feeds the squirrels all winter long,

Bellies full, leaping from limb to limb, singing a squirrel song.

At night, I am the sentry, watching over my human's home.

I believe I'm their favorite; when they talk, it's in their tone.

Like them getting a haircut, they give me a trim.

I'm so proud; I, too, have a deep soul within.

I'm happy to do my part for human society.

I'm a member of nature, hosting animals and my deity.

There's a crow coming for a landing.
It's my old pal Andy!
"Hey, Andy, clean out your damn nest. It's full of junk!
I'm an oak tree in good standing; you're jeopardizing my trunk.
Do you see that guy watching us? What will he think
When his beautiful property starts to stink?"

The observer ended his curious gaze of the tree and crow.
"Hey, Nancy, do you believe trees have a soul?"

Jets Wilson Jewel

He's young and on fire—24 to be exact.

In plain sight of the sparrows and crows,

On a Tennessee Walker, he's galloping along the track,

Kicking up black dirt from the railbed as he goes.

He's wild like the horse, proudly sitting high in the saddle,

There is no heaven; there is no hell.

His heart and the horse's are pumping life's purest blood.

There's nothing more and nothing less powerful of joy to tell.

If you love freedom, when you ride you'll be understood.

A runner at 30, the wind in his face, running like his old horse,

Sending precious oxygen through his arteries and veins.

He is life; he is wild and intoxicated with his life's course.

Faster is his pace; longer is his stride; he's a poet's refrain.

He feels so much love for the memory of the horse.

He and that horse never wanted to be reined.

As time has swiftly passed them both by,

All he ever needed was the love of a horse to get high!

Act Four

It was a long sleep; his eyes opened slowly.

And the show was over.

The curtain opened, and all the cast was on the stage, bowing.

By the time the closing act ended, he was sober.

As the cast were doffing their sartorial costumes

And cleansing their makeup and stage perfumes

After congratulating each other,

A new play was in order.

The news came to all by a man with a jaded look,

"Go home now and rest; there will come another."

The promise came years later while reading a new book,

Even though he and the cast were all older.

This could be the final play to be booked?

Or is it time for them to be put out to pasture and graze?

Is he still in the audience awakening from a dream nap?

Was it just a dream and was he still in a daze?

Or perhaps an illusion that he was the main character,
Performing and being applauded, alone on the stage.

His eyes were at half lid as he realized he was not an actor.
There was no play, no stage, no cast, just his misty stare.
A smell of urine and a feces-full bedpan at his side.
A final performance in a nursing home and sadly aware!

What Do You See?

There was this man sitting by the rear of a car.
As I passed by him, he signaled for me to talk.
Being a friendly guy, I noticed his guitar,
He leaned toward my ear and said, "I can't walk.

Understand it's all my fault; it's the life I've lived.
I drank all the whiskey and beer I could find,
And I started using drugs to help me survive,
So, sir, would you do this one thing for me?

Look into my heart and tell me what you see,
How much darkness or light?
Am I evil or could it be
I'm not too bright?"

"Well, sir, I don't want to reject your request,
But in as much as your heart has continued to beat,
It's more about what you don't seem to know.
So, let me be honest and tell you, this is what I see:
You must forget about your heart and look into your
soul."

Merry Christmas Morgan Chase & Co.

It was the night before Christmas, and all through the town,

Homes were decorated with bright red, blue, and green Christmas light.

Dinner tables were laden with select gourmet foods,

And setting next to roasted ham, candelabras signaling affluence burned bright.

People of all faiths poured onto the nocturnal snow-covered streets,

Midnight mass was over, and rosy-cheeked Christians shouted, "Merry Christmas, everyone!"

All seemed happy and cordial, even the cats were fed, and every pet dog had a special wrapped bone.

Unbeknown to all those well fed happy people in their beautifully decorated homes, across town in a rundown shack, a very sick old man sat alone.

He had nothing much to eat, just some leftover beans and a piece of cheese.

His love for God was real, his belly was empty, but his soul wasn't thinking of a savior's birth.

But rather the cruelty of his death, and how quietly he cried.

So, while the Christians were seated at their festive tables, stuffing their guts and saluting the birth of baby Jesus, drinking the best wines money could buy,

The sick, old man had a single candle glowing in the room of his rundown shack,

Aware his own death was not too far away.

Unable to buy his meds, he thought of the greedy men who had Jesus crucified.

Not as though this old man was alone, suffering abject circumstances, a little further down near the railroad tracks dwelled many less fortunate than him who were shivering in tarp-covered shacks.

So, this night of kindness and cheer will end tomorrow.

All the celebrators of goodwill and cheer will have another drink before their hatred and greed come back.

So, all the Christmas story ads watched on television and carols sung on radio sold billions of dollars on toys for children, made more money than they could count.

And the truth of it appeared in the bank statements all around the globe, exposing a bullshit story exploited by the false prophets about the sermon on the mount.

What if just maybe the goodwill, joy, and happiness

Was the truth among all men on the globe

Instead of the thousands of castle-like churches where

Behind alter podiums were the anointed preaching for more of the working man's gold,

While they were hiding behind a crucified man's robe.

I am also among those who ask why God has failed to conquer evil.

If the hearts of men were really full of goodwill, what a wonderful world it would be.

But the reality of what we do to each other from day to day tells us goodwill is safely in the bank. Goodwill doesn't apply to the sick, hungry, and now-on-the-planet born or unborn babies.

If you want all of those cozy, wonderful goodwill things, I'm afraid you'll have to wait until next Christmas, or Easter, if boiled eggs and chocolate rabbits are your thing.

Coming soon: Hypocrisy in the choir.

How angelically they all sing.

It's a Boy

From the womb, he was expelled into the hands of a midwife's anxiety.

Counting 10 fingers and toes, a whole baby being was now among society.

It was a pure, innocent challenge of a new baby's first day of life.

Surrounded by gift giving, well wishing family, and for a wife's nine months of anxiety.

Now begins the unknown journey into a human world of love and hate.

Bathed, fed, clothed, and covered warmly in his new crib.

As he sleeps, all the ignorant failures in his orbit are already planning his fate.

Mother's and father's vicarious competition arrives ever so stealthily.

"Oh, my God," says Mother. "He has my nose!" "Yes," says Dad. "But he looks more like me!"

In the house of euphoria, adults were acting thrillingly.

With strong, solicitous demands, the father asks relatives, "Can't you see?"

50

The radio was playing the new hit song in 1937, "I've Got Your Love to Keep Me Warm."

So, the years passed, and everyone went to their office, factory, or farm.

The boy went through all the usual stages, trying hard to learn.

The schools he went to couldn't explain the boy's disorder.

Although formal academics wasn't his thing, the street was.

Expelled from school, his parents were notified by court order.

Authorities were liberal and lenient with the law.

His mother was his mother, but his father wasn't his father, he was later told.

He, along with many other kids, was a victim of a growing trend.

Somehow, he made it through life and slowly grew old.

The boy did well for himself in life but avoided making too many friends.

Some people would look at him as if they knew.

He didn't need their looks, but he always wondered if it was true.

In spite of all that was right or wrong in his life, it was still special in a way.

Yet through it all, he suspected an empty spot was in his chest, a hole.

Despite all the journeys and the things people would do and say,

In a flash of enlightenment, he realized his ultimate goal.

One night while asleep in his bed, an angel relayed,

"What you've been searching for all your life is your soul.

Your soul is what in that hole in your chest must go!"

His father was eventually found in a prison for crimes that he must pay.

It wasn't what the boy needed to hear when a father was needed to help him grow.

Accustomed to a life of disappointment, it still closed the hole.

Today, he's at peace, loving the sight of crow!

Recall

Aware of growing limitations, you struggle to recall a name.

A name of a person you interacted with in a significant way.

And you're angry because it's too soon for an aging brain.

You mention your concern, wanting to hear them say

They don't notice any difference, "You're okay."

While sheltering the honest lie and agree but fail to see.

A good night's sleep, you're up and out and say,

"Gather, my lovely dog and cats, now do you agree?

It's just too much on my mind that was building every day."

A field of golden wheat, with the patterns of gold it makes.

As the wind blows across its unharvested lakes of hay,

Trying to hold onto lucidity for whatever effort it takes.

Getting old can't be faked.

"Wait a second, those pain pills this morning, did I take?

I remember I had them in my hand, or was that yesterday?"

I won't tell anyone, for it's an issue they might make.

I'll pretend I took them, and maybe the pain won't be as bad today.

Outside, the angry wind is slapping the rain against my windowpane.

In a loud whisper, it seems to repeatedly say, "Ignore your pain. Ignore your pain. Ignore your pain."

Looking in the mirror, when suddenly to me it came.

Goddamn it! I knew I'd remember. His name: It was James.

Now the leaves are falling like my hair,

And it's almost the end of September.

But those pills, those freaking pills. I did or didn't take them?

Well, maybe tomorrow, I won't need to walk with a cane, if I remember!

Whispers in Your Ear

There's someone whispering in your ear.

Not wanting to hear the awful things,

You turn away out of fear.

Could it be true? The things they are saying are so pitiful.

There is someone whispering an ominous warning.

There's danger ahead for you. If you fail to listen, you may lose your head.

From persistent warning, you fail to heed, your guard comes down.

Instead, you think you're learning the truth.

Your heart is still beating, but your soul is dead.

From far away, in some secluded, quiet place.

The whispers are heard loud and clear when face to face.

The whispering voice goes into hiding.

As time passes by, and the whispers fade away.

But the heart and soul damage stay.

While the love that once was remains,

Injured by what the liar had to say.

Sometimes revived by the lyrics in a popular song.

The reality of damaged whispers are not long gone.

What he said was so shameful,

And certainly not right.

However, in the end, watch out for someone

Too close, who you think of as a friend.

It's Raining

Shh, I'm listening for the sound love makes in the rain.

Streetlights glisten in the rain like tinsel on a Christmas tree.

A wind wildly blowing, young, a full head of dark hair.

Rain becomes a downpour, and I'm walking without a care.

Listening and hoping for the rhythmic sound of who I used to be.

This thing I do, I guess I'm trying to find my way back to me.

In my heart lurks the brightnesss of love and the darkness of pain.

With all the listening and all the wind and rain.

It tells me new flowers will bloom,

And some new trees will grow.

There'll be more of the me's just like me, who will come and who will go.

Listen closely to the unyielding truth, and you will hear.

"I'll never be me again," and now that the rain has slowed

Deaf silence will consume tomorrow when it's clear.

Without the pouring rain, there's nothing more to hear.

I won't be listening!

Grief

Somehow, someway, I'll make it through this day.

With no lingering sadness

Obstructing any leftover madness

From that awful news of yesterday.

There once was a mountain I climbed,

Which had a breathtaking view below.

Standing in awe of the sight, I felt enlightened

And started again to spiritually grow.

Now in these trembling hands,

A tear touches the cablegram.

It smears the worst words of all, "I'm sorry, Madam."

"Your husband won't be coming home," continued the devastating gram.

"His heart gave out,

And he didn't make it through.

Just before he expired, he whispered

That he always loved you."

Unable to stand, I sat and cried, asking, "Why, my
God?
So high up in the sky, why, oh why, did you let my
loving man die?
Shall I fall to my knees and pray it's only a dream
And wake up, knowing it was all a dreamer's lie?

Tomorrow, I'll go to the mountaintop,
Which now is covered with white, virgin snow.
Yes, dear God, that's where I must go to slowly heal
My heart and soul and watch the melting snow."

Affirming her goal, she rose from the table.
Dropping to the floor was the cable.

Listen

While Zamfir plays "Amazing Grace" on his flute
Cradled and embraced in his frail arms,
Shivering, my memories float.
His music transports me without alarm.

To thoughts of what's left of my tomorrow.
Enraptured tears find their way from my soul
Realize all I've ever been.
There was no sorrow.

With less tomorrows, in many ways,
I am thankful for all the yesterdays.
I see God's crimson sunset on a tranquil sea.
I see my seven angels hovering over me.

I've lived a sweet life, lived free.
As beautiful and free as it has been for me,
Is now my wish for all
Of those who follow me.

Tears for a Tree

Save some of those tears for another day.

You cried an ocean for the loves you lost.

You thought your sadness would never go away.

The nights were sleepless; tears fell on your own cross.

Get a grip; there's more sadness coming your way.

Hearts again will break; they're not made of clay.

Someone close who you know will pass away.

You'll need more of those tears that you save.

Then comes a day while answering the phone,

You clearly understand the day when all of us will be gone.

The phone will ring; someone else is in your old home.

And in life's end, crying won't right the wrong.

In the time designated from above,

Nothing will remain on Earth, not a man nor a dove.

Then understand the tears shed by me

Should've, after all, been saved for a tree.

A Tree and Me

"Good morning, Mr. Evergreen Tree,

I humbly apologize for all the years I've been ignorantly lacking in manners."

"You should be. I've been standing here as plain as could be,

Giving you a beautiful daily view of nature to feed your cultural soul, as well as for all the neighborhood to see.

Now that we have broken the ice, would you mind shaking the snow out of my bottom limb?

Thank you, Mr. Man, now some of my training chicks out there will be able to fly back in.

You know, sir, I've been seeing you more than you've been seeing me.

I noticed the other day as you hurried by, you looked so sad and tears in your eyes, I could see.

Is there something you would like to share? I know I'm just a tree,

But I can keep a secret. Anyway, who would believe a talking tree?"

"Thank you, but I'm not ready to explain emotions that come and go in my dreams.

Since we're now on speaking terms, may I ask, how many nests are resting on your boughs?"

"Too many for the moment. It seems that I may need more branches so more chicks can move in now!

As you well know, I'm a Norwegian Spruce by name.

You planted me in November, and like you, I'm a Scorpio.

I'm passionate, and like some of those scrub oak trees, I'm not easy to please because I need room to grow.

Sir, there's something I've been wondering about. Is that a Sassafras one tree away from me?

He sits quietly through the seasons. No bird ever lands on him, he seems so lonely.

He's the last one among us to bloom in the spring

And the last to drop his leaves in the fall. What's his thing?"

"Maybe in his heart, he's embarrassed

And likes to hang around a little longer in the spring.

Perhaps he holds onto his green longer in the fall

So, when the other trees are bare, he'll be the prettiest
of all."

"I guess you're right about that.

I'm happy, but too deeply rooted to ever walk.

Just kidding, sir, but you know

That neither of us is good with small talk."

Questionable Sorrow

To all the crows that can't fly,

For all the hungry deer in the winter wood,

And all the awesome wonders of the sky,

For all the deprived kids in the old neighborhood.

They, as am I, and I, as are they.

Ever so long ago, on the streets where we played to have fun,

Unlike many Ukraine streets covered with blood

Where the children of war are deprived of care and the dignity of evil men's love.

Some children, the crows they will never see fly

And will only see animals starving in the woods.

All the beautiful birds with brains the size of a pea,

Yet have souls bigger than the evil three.

Russia, Philippines, and Turkey.

Who am I, who never suffered pain

And been regularly fed, to feel deprived?

Who am I to complain?

Oh, dear Lord, on my porch a package has arrived.

Peacock Blues

I have become envious of the other peacocks in the coop.

They have all their plumage yet to display.

While I lost too many feathers and feel like a dope.

I was sick, and they put some awful medicine in my hay.

So, I may be staying inside for a long, long time.

And never again have a proud plumage to display.

"Be satisfied for the full dress" that once was mine.

Is what the other, young peacocks always say.

Doesn't make it easier, when they're just being kind.

Oh, how I am saddened by their proud, beautiful strut.

The truth is, I had my day. It's not their fault I'm old.

This cage, this awful cage, like me is showing rust.

It could be worse, if to the poultry store, I'm sold.

Unless a rejuvenation revives my bright blue and green,

I'll roost and watch the females choose a handsome mate.

While the glory of my broken-down body again won't be seen.

Too old to feel, too old to heal, and too old to procreate.

Oddly true, everything about bird, man, or beast is planned from above.

As the senses all by design age and dim

The one thing of all that remains indestructible is true love.

Whether by walk, crawl, fly, or swim,

It's the last of her or him.

I am a noble, old peacock, who lost its blue and green.

I once would leave the cage and display what my bird God gave to me.

But now the sweetest miracle for a bird like me,

Is to wake from a dream, be dead, and still dream.

Lady Peacock Blues

Alone in the darkest of nights, inside the deepest canyon

As she sleeps, her controls are deep, in the depth of its subconscious.

Continuous recurrence of that one thought, the echoing goes on.

Endlessly, it comes back as if in an unrelenting permanent trance.

As the overtures were meant to demean or assure her of a tomorrow,

Those echoes from within that daunting portending ominous canyon

Are meant to pierce her young, tender heart to bear much sorrow.

Awake and light-footed, she walks cautiously and talks with confusion and without abandon.

Once someone spoke to her of a bird that couldn't fly,

"What?" I think. "Whatever does it mean?

What does it have to do with those echoes I hear?"

Some nights anxiously I hurry back to my sleep to dream.

The darker the night, the deeper down the canyon she goes.

I am in the bottom, looking up at a comet's flash-by stream.

I, too, am a young, wounded bird who wants to grow old.

Wisdom, hope, and glory were the echoing words I've been told.

I'm a wounded but proud peacock.

But I won't be sold!

Not to any uncaring butcher who doesn't give a damn.

Despite those veiled echoes, I still love who I am!

A Used-to-Be Man

Everything about me is a used-to-be man

And nothing of what I am today.

Looking around for a space to relax with my memories,

Gladly gone are the productive years; all that remains are confused vagaries.

Worried always of what stupid people would say,

I would rush to be whatever fate planned for me to be.

Never feeling a need to pray.

Dirty hands, face, and feet, runny nose and bad teeth

But yet, always red, rosy cheeks.

The neighborhood kids on the block

Went to catechism, learned all about church and God.

While I stayed away and sat on a rock.

I learned to shoot and steal fruit,

While they received sacraments and were entered in a log.

Following the path, most kids went on to acquire a degree.

They did well, yet I was an optimist,

71

Never cared to plan things too far ahead.

I was on a wild spree.

As is the tendency of old men like me, looking back on the path I casually chose.

Most of the people who were significant in my transient life are now in a forever snooze.

As a used-to-be man, at the age of 84, I can hear the lyrics,

"You are my sunshine," and then will stop singing the blues.

I guess by now,

There should be a final verse.

Well, fuck it.

I never did like to rehearse!

Cabin Fever

Did someone in the crowd mention cabin fever?

Well, let me out!

A crowd of guys and tough-looking gals

Were drinking whiskey, shouting as loud as they could shout.

They were rude and disturbing the peace, except for the one who left his cabin just to get out.

They were feeling falsely free from a prison they were never in, but soon a real jail cell they may see.

The crowd kept growing, and the more of them there were, the louder they demanded to be free.

The group was rudderless, but the loudest mouth assumed control, claiming he had the key.

Silence swept over the crowd as he proclaimed he would open that prison that they were never in.

Shouting morphed to quieter rumbling by those who were for and against him.

A calmer, formidable man moved forward, signaling to be heard.

And he was allowed to begin.

The crowd settled to hear what this calm man had to say.

"Friends, this gathering was unintentional. We didn't meet somewhere in secret for a cause or pledge to obey.

Look above! See the clear sky and the intoxicating moon and its stars so bright.

We came here with our beer, whiskey, and gin, intent on having fun, not to riot or fight.

Look at the man next to you and around to the others and observe what you see.

There are no handcuffs, chains, nor physical restraints.

We're not in jail.

We're all free."

A sobering attitude calmed the crowd as some started walking away.

The loudest mouth, who said he had the key, finished the whiskey in his flask and called it a day.

When the crowd was gone, it was all about nothing, never a reason to rant, rave, and shout.

Except for that one man with cabin fever, saying to himself, "All I wanted was just to get out!"

Justice

Can you hear it? It's coming your way!
It's a storm loaded with the ashes of yesterday.
All your dreams and treasures will be carried away.
It's time to get on your knees and pray.

Those cocktail dinners, meetings with filet and steak,
All those excuses for the overnights you make.
It's coming your way. Can you hear the storm?
Get ready, be ready. It's far from the norm.
The cheating, lying, and stealing, now you must face.
The judges are paneled and all in their place.

In the eye of the storm, you'll surely be,
When quickly, you are pronounced *guilty*.
The storm, loaded with the ashes of yesterday,
Is coming to carry your guilty ass away.

A Bridge

There was a bridge of 40 miles in span,

Built by people who dreamed of the other side.

On one side was hope,

On the other, solid land.

On that bridge was a darkness,

Where some men died.

There was a crowd who cursed the darkness,

And they cried,

"Burn the bridge down!"

But still, some hoped there would be light on the other side.

The bridge now stands, connecting town with town.

Yet the bridge burners are still around, suborning anyone who'll listen to their tired, old dark song.

When the advocates who see the prevailing light,

Reflect on the bridge's 40 years and its miles long,

It's still standing. It must be right.

That isn't wrong.

Act of Bravery or Torture

He's a beautifully donned man,

With a sword in his hand,

Plunges it deep into the charging bull's heart.

Then listens to the wild cheers from the adoring arena crowd.

The bleachers are full of blood-thirsty bullfight fans, vicariously filling their own unfulfilled lives.

"Bravo, bravo, torero," louder and louder they shout as he proudly waves his red cape and bows.

He doesn't leave the arena until the adoring crowd is satisfied,

And the peons dutifully enter with a truck to haul the carcass off the blood-soaked sand.

The truck is loaded with tagged bulls destined for the slaughterhouse.

My presence defined incongruity as I cheered for the bull and became the arena louse.

Witnessing cruelty to animals isn't bravery deserving of glory from a thundering applause by blood-hungry fans.

It's the ceremonial execution of an innocent animal created by God and placed on this land.

What honor and glory are given to the bull,
Who didn't have the chance, cape, nor sword to
tantalize and kill the man?
The bull wasn't conquered as in a fair sport.
It was cowardly murdered.

Swords of brave men with red capes in hand,
Committing acts of bravery and honored
Is not a venerable sport. It's a public display of
butchery.
Watching the bull's blood tracks as it's drug from the
arena's sand,

I wondered if their God thinks it's okay to slay?
To slaughter His animals in this way?
What does a brave man's heart, designed by the God
We are baptized to obey, silently say?

Instead, he ignores the ethereal echoes.
He expels them from his head.
And he continues to sharpen his sword
To kill, until every last bull is dead.

A bull-cheering arena louse, I shook my head and thought, "When will God define heroism and bravery?

If killing is displayed as bravery, what can the definition of cruelty and torture of animals be?"

A beautiful, black raven flew over the excited crowd.

But no one looked up, except me.

Highest High

When the sun warms my entire body and my feet are in wonderment while caressing the Earth,

Where upon the feet of all others have also touched in search

For the place where all lovers met,

Feeling their past and futures together, never to regret.

The search ends with a gentle whispering wind that calms each undaunted soul.

And I am whole. I am finally whole.

All of God's waters entering my heart, I am in harmony

With all his wonderful living things.

As such, my love for all creation is now in tune

With the meaning of flower and tree blooming in the month of June.

And with all the tears of sadness and all the smiles of joy

In each epoch moment that are felt in the heart of this man/boy.

Using hundreds of words that will never explain

All my life's mysterious pain

About a love of life during its highest high

Filling all five lobes with oxygen that money can't buy.

Yesterday's Child

World War II was over, and in towns and cities
everywhere,

People were celebrating in the streets.

A triumphant America won renewed hope

For its people and the people's right to vote.

One late August day, his knees on a pavement

A boy merely eight years of age,

Applies polish to a returning veteran's tan shoes.

The boy's brown eyes were like freshly polished
jewels.

Glowing joy upon his boyish face,

With his youthful, uncombed hair all over the place,

Happily, shines the shoes of the soldier

Without understanding or knowing what purpose in
life he, too, would serve with dignity and grace.

He felt life in every beat of his young heart.

He was happy and felt God upon his shoulders.

Contentedly, he worked the rhythm of his brush and
rag.

All he wanted to do was give the best shoeshine; he
didn't brag.

Proudly earning some money to help his mom and
unemployed dad,
He never felt deprived or saddened by his lot.
He felt cheerful, privileged, and blessed
Because he's needed, and in a trade, he's been taught.

In his pockets, the 10-cent and nickel tips grew into
dollars and more
Until, finally, he was sure
He had enough to share
With his waiting mother.

Upon finishing his shoeshine route,
He closed his shine box with tools of the trade in place.
And his kind, privileged heart,
To his home, he would race.

He shouted to be heard everywhere,
"Look, Mom, what I've earned, look here."
The young, red-haired mother of six, grateful for her
share,

Hugged her young entrepreneur.

But that was a long time ago.
The images fade; they come, and they go.
The shoeshine boy, now a man in his eighties,
Misses his mom and dad.

But he knows they're gone,
And he'll never see them again
Well, maybe?

Wiping the tears flowing over his wrinkled cheek,
He recalls how happy he was,
Pleasing his mom,
While shining shoes of men in the city street.

Those men, never knowing what their nickels and
dimes meant
To the young boy shining their shoes back then.
That was when a victorious nation loved its people
Whose fighting on blood-soaked foreign sands freed
people around the globe.

In today's child, with modern rearing standards
He would be an abused victim of parental abuse.
Contacting the ACLU,
His parents, they would sue.

I still hear the "Pop, pop, pop, whack,"
As a soldier would say, "Don't forget the back!"
This old man lovingly smiled,
Recalling what it's like to be yesterday's child.

It Was Only a Dream

As I arose from last night's summer dream,
No ill will appears in this morning's theme.
That's all it was:
Just a wishful dream.

About life, not much of anything, nothing to know.
And now to a blank sheet of paper, whiter than snow.
Like an artist's canvas,
Waiting for his talent to show.

Like the last days of an autumn sun,
Chances are it will never get done.

From my window glared by the west-setting sun
Some bared branches on the maple tree tell me
That ominous shadows beyond the acorns of
A neighboring oak tree: Winter is near.

And there it is, not in a dream but vivid reality.
The magnificent gold and crimson colors of fall are so
clear,

A Heart Searching for Its Soul

As in my November heart and soul there dwells a
lasting tranquility.

So, as in the changes of all things.

There is both some joy and some sorrow.

As we enter into winter, we're already dreaming of
next spring.

Sadly, some will and others will not be here tomorrow.

Sing, cardinal, sing. Sing blue bird, sing. In chorus, all
birds sing.

Everyone, sing those songs you all know,

While we're waiting for next spring's flowers to grow.

The Last Song

The moon lights the night,

The sun warms the day,

And stars guide our way.

Tonight, celestial harpists will strum their gentle chords,

While angelic choirs sitting upon heavenly clouds

Softly echo these whispering words,

"It's going to be alright. There'll be no dark clouds or bloody swords."

Not a mortal being, nor the Lord almighty,

Shall fear the living and conclude rightly

Not so much of our own death or however begotten

Is being remembered and too soon forgotten.

The sin of sins of never having been is a haunting sorrow:

That all relationships, we only borrow.

And when the fear of fears—death—become clear,

It's only with family we'll be remembered here.

So, behold my dear,

A day will come when the last child closes the door.

Then it won't be long until we're all gone.

And the ocean tide will no longer touch the shore.

As you listen tonight,

Sing with the angels all the songs your heart can hold,

Before it ends,

And your story is never told.

Don't Ask Why

A simple man,

Who as a child was warmed by the sun.

A warm heart,

A heart of many being one.

Alone yet not alone,

His shadow and a passing bird's were flung,

As mysterious silhouettes on the moon,

A waiting world tries to unlock the mystery of where
it all begun.

The secret no living man has ever found or revealed,

The why or how a universe is done

The same journey,

Made by so many others' fruitless ordeals.

All of whom found nothing but a closed door,

An inquiry, ended as it begun and nothing more.

In the end, the shadow of the child and bird are sure

The whys are beyond what we see of the moon and
Jupiter.

If the story of this life remains a celestial secret,

And death fails to silence hearts and souls, so be it.

Everything about this life while here in form, even
from above,

Save for the only true faith of being in love.

Dead will receive the dead,

Into their eternal arms to hold.

And, in passing, the child once warmed by the sun

Will have no fear of being cold.

Who Am I?

Who am I?
Who am I in the comfort of my home
To sit idly by
And watch the Ukrainians die?

Who am I?
Who am I with a bitch and a moan
About gas prices and pathetically cry,
"What can be done?"

You easily say, "I care, but I'm not over there.
Why should Americans have to pay?
It's their own people who need to fight.
Why should I pay more for gas at the pump?
If their freedom is our freedom,
Would that be right?"

Who am I?
Who am I in the comfort of my home
To feel nothing while Ukrainians die?
To turn away from looking when a baby's guts are
blown.

"What can I do?" asks the man, licking chicken off a
bone.

Who am I?

Who am I who will glory in their spunk.

When the war is over, and freedom is won?

I was in their corner all the time,

And I knew they wouldn't be sunk.

Who am I?

Who am I in the warmth of a new March sun

To plan my day at the shopping mall.

Blind to suffering mothers and fathers

Who need no sympathy but our bullets and our gun.

Who am I?

Who am I who is deaf to sacrifice's call,

While eating a cheesesteak hoagie at the mall.

"Hey, Marty, did you hear again gas is going to go
up?"

"Jesus Christ, enough is enough."

Who are we?

Who are we, so divided a people

Putting party ahead of its country?

So lacking in national pride,

With a vacant look when our child asks, "Daddy, what is genocide?"

Will I Know?

Will I ever know when it's the last word I'll write,

Under that last night of darkness and dreams

Or those sunny days with dimming light

And all the rivers become silent downstream?

What will it be, that last word that I write?

What letter will it be, between an A and a Z?

Before comes the day when I have nothing more to
write or to say,

Let me get this out of the way.

I never wanted anything that wasn't mine

All I ever wanted is what God has given to me:

Two eyes for love

And a little glass of wine.

All I ever needed to be happy was the simple things:

The natural colors of trees in the early fall,

And the scent of lilies in the spring.

Oh, those girls with long hair that falls

And innocent passion their young hearts bring

What is it that I haven't written?
What is it that my shame won't let me tell?
What have I kept inside and never given?
This is my heaven; my lies are my hell.

To show so much love for the black-feathered crow,
Is it my soul I hid so deep inside?
Was it the rain or the wind or the winter snow?
Was it my secret heart that lied when it cried?
Or was it just a man with false pride.

Will I ever know that last word I'll live to write?
Will I have the courage to give it up without a fight?
I never wanted anything that wasn't mine.
I always had my precious eyesight.
Like fresh grapes from the vine,
Have I been just an elusive actor in a bad show?
I really do not want to know!

Will I ever know if I did all that I could?
In a world of many a great achiever,
Was my time understood
As a non-believer?

Each Season with You

It's the blue lights of Christmas I miss in July,

And the warmth of summer that puts tears in my old eye.

It's the first look into your eyes as I remember their glow

Was between winter and summer or was it fall's gold?

It's the blue sparkle of tinsel on the Christmas trees,

And the songs of each season that play in my heart of our memories.

It's the emerald green of that first May 7th that I miss in my dreams

And the white night of December's gifts of love that Christmas brings.

It's the splendor of color, the magic of a topaz ring, and the autumn leaves' song I used to sing.

And the scent of lilies drawing my passion into memories of a first kiss that one night brings

A little bit of those past happenings in the passing seasons of every life.

It's the reality of living through all the younger years to find the special jewels between husband and wife.

All the seasons of passing years have only been worthy of our harmony

Because your strength made them more meaningful to me.

It's the blue lights of Christmas I miss in July,

And the emerald beauty I saw in your May 7th Taurus eye.

You've been through so much, believe it or not.

You'll always be the emerald-eyed beauty I met and kissed in Dino's lot.

Happy anniversary!

Your Blood, Their Glory

I dismissed myself as a serious man.
How unworthy I must be, without knowing their plan.
I must be unworthy if I misinterpreted their intent.
Surely, it makes me a malcontent.

But what I suspect is a prejudiced evaluation
Of an evil man who's holding a gun
Is defenseless against the man
Who had the bullets in his hand.

So, I let the sun shine this morn,
With all its brilliance upon my weary bones.
And I listen to the pundits' moans,
Competing with others' mission to scorn.

I hear the assurances of candidates wanting to lead,
Telling us, you and I, that it's okay to bleed,
To surrender our hopes, to give up our dreams
And to drain our blood for their need.

In real time, a Republican candidate
For governor of PA did arrogantly proclaim

Sans disgrace, no hesitate,
Claims he's sent by Trump without shame.

Again, I dismiss myself as a serious man
For wondering who's this man who thinks he's the
people's hope.
Sent by a liar who never presented a plan
To represent us before we vote.

The arrogance grows in our nation laden with sorrow.
A shameless man, who wants it all, will be on the
ballot.
I'm wondering how we'll feed our kids tomorrow,
Fearing how much the voters will swallow.

I'm a simple man. Is my gun a right to vote?
What's it mean if they decide where my vote goes?
Truly, I must be unworthy to promote
More guns for us and fewer guns for those.

A gullible Republican, chosen by Trump to save PA,
Let's all hope the voters' guns are all loaded
Enough to send this arrogant bullshitter away,
By the people's truth who vote.

Born Again

Good morning, new day.

I'm awake and ready to play.

I'm so happy to greet you.

I've so many things still to do,

Left over from yesterday.

Out of the rain and into the sun,

The race will begin,

Without shots from a starter's gun.

It will be great, this day number one.

Out of the rain and into the sun,

Every woman will be a queen; every man has a crown.

The face of every citizen will don a smile

Good morning, new day, hope you'll be here for a while.

Out of the darkness and into the light,

A new day, another chance to make things right.

Good morning, new day, I'll plant an elderberry bush and a brand-new tree,

Then end this new morning happily.

As the morning gives way to the July noon,
I'll dine on the berries that grew this June.
Throughout this new midday, I'll sing and write
And prepare my soul for a peaceful night.

I'll dream of a quiet street,
Where children are asleep.
In a better world, on this new day
That we were meant to keep.

Watching Genocide

While the open eyes of the world are watching,
A mass murderer commits genocide,
Blasting bombs on civilians, whose only capacity
Is to fight with their unwavering pride.

"It's unfair," the world declares.
America, divided, trying to save its own democracy,
Proclaims to the UN with pious hypocrisy.
"We'll sanction to slow their aggression and go after
their billionaires!"

Meanwhile our own billionaires and millionaires
Are not paying their fair share at home.
And the press reports on the slaughter
As a daily show.

The United Nations offers up more sanctions,
As the bodies of wives, sons, and daughters
Die in the arms of their loved ones,
Regardless of the world's reactions.

The madness and murderous mind of one man,

Destroys a nation in front of the world's eyes.

While we watch, declaring, "We're doing all we can,"

The criminal continues to murder, and to his own people, he lies.

The war crimes continue despite sanctions in place.

Glued to the news are countries next to be invaded.

As cries of the people shout louder, "It's a disgrace."

"What are we waiting for? Capture the madman holding the world hostage," they say, frustrated.

Where are all the mercenaries? Did they disappear

To holiday bunkers for the war-weary and jaded?

What will it take to unravel the fear?

Of a war criminal, a mass murderer so near

To the Romanian and Finland borders?

Could this, should this be

A lesson for us all to hear?

A war criminal, the dictator of one nation, vast in empty territory,

A little man whose manic profile of narcissism is secretly trembling

Wants Ukrainian blood for his glory.

From the people, not their leaders, comes a clarion call,

"One brave nation fights to save freedom and democracy for us all!'

It remains the duty of the United Nations

Not to drop the ball.

Sanctions are not enough to stop the war criminal's bombs and bullets.

That he's been shootin.'

The world must capture and prosecute

This war criminal named Putin.

And while we're doing all of this

To support a vulnerable nation save its treasured democracy,

Let's protect ourselves from those here without national patriotic pride,

The ones, we fear, seek only to divide.

The First and Last Light

The stars never shined so bright as in the eyes of a child who sees them for the first time.

The moon never held as much mystery and excitement as in the eyes of a young boy.

The sun never felt so warm as in the first hot summer of a child's first trip to the shore.

The child grows into an adult and does whatever he does, some become poets, look at the stars they try to define.

A mature man is tantalized by the moon with his never-ending challenge to enjoy.

The white boy as a man pits his body against the sun's rays to get tanned and always craving more.

A teenager's first kiss is never as life-defining as is the pursuit of it again.

A mother's first born is held more tightly, like nothing she ever held before.

A father's first look at his daughter or son gives him purpose and manhood.

The journey of everyone through the path lit by the sun's light is a guide, which can't be restrained.

A mother's child becomes an adult and must leave through an open door.

As for the father, his journey is his pride, which he never really understood.

The father, mother, son, and daughter all grow old.

Eventually, they see the stars, moon, and sun for the last time.

From the shiny beginnings of life and everything we learned to hold dear,

To see and love is the message so clear, "Don't waste a second! Enjoy it while you're here."

As those once bright eyes grow tired and dim,

Like when a candlewick's last flame burns out,

No matter how much you scream or shout,

It can't be lit again.

It's Sunday in America

Outside my window, the sun is shining bright.

March has come to assert its volatile power of change.

Meanwhile in Russia, there sits a man so deranged,

With a small, sovereign nation, he picks a fight.

It's Sunday morning in America,

And the buds will soon be on the tree.

My home is warm and cozy; we're free.

Soon the flowers will share their sweet scent of erotica.

It's Sunday morning in America,

While here at home, it's a Sunday tradition

To give thanks for all our freedom and human rights,

Fought for by minorities in Alabama.

America protects what's theirs as a sole mission,

But in Ukraine, bombs and missiles

Terrorize the brave people,

Who vow to Russia there'll be no submission.

It's Sunday morning in America,

Breakfast is on the table with its bacon smell.

As the news shocks us of the attack on Horlivka,
Suddenly the bacon and eggs smell like hell.

It's Sunday morning in Ukraine,
A sovereign democratic nation,
Where men, women, and children, far too young die.
No church bells are ringing, and the people are war
weary, too weak to cry.

It's Sunday morning in America,
Spring is upon us, with the hope of a new everything.
As the bombs are destroying the city of Horodyna,
Their people are in bunkers, praying.

It's Sunday morning in America,
We're still free to hope, play, and plan,
But when a Ukrainian soldier or civilian dies,
Their world is ended; they no longer can.

It's Sunday morning in America,
Rapidly closing freedom's moat.
My America, your America, together with Ukraine,
That's the sword of autocracy at our throat.

What Ya Gonna Do?

A detached father would always say,
"What ya gonna do? It's the way things are today."

Listening close by is a boy who has no toy,
But a head full of dark, brown hair.
He knew it wasn't fair,
But he pretended he didn't care.

Every night under the moonlight,
At the stars he'd stare
And wonder about God,
While contemplating life so fair.

Does He really care
About a boy who has no toy?
And by the river he'd go,
To watch the water flow.

And as the story goes,
It became a way of life.
Too young, but he fell in love
And then he took a wife.

Then two children they had:
One a girl, one a boy.
Even if they were bad,
They both had too many a toy.

The years, they have swiftly gone by.
The man no longer looks for answers,
About life and love in the sky.
In precious speeding time, he found all the things we
need are right here on the ground.

As a new age father today, he whispers in their ear,
"Come over here and hear!"
And then he would smile and say,
"What ya gonna do? It's the way things are today!"

Those Were the Days

There was a time when children walked to school.

That was the horse-and-buggy day.

When parents and teachers taught the golden rule

Kids learned the ABCs and also about fair play.

There was a time when schools didn't have delays.

Kids walked in snow, half a five-year-old's size.

They played to and from, until they were home

How wet they were, they didn't realize.

There was a time when streets weren't plowed.

All milk was delivered by horse-drawn wagons, but horseshit on the streets wasn't allowed.

Behind each horse's tail and butt was a tarpaulin trap,

Designed to catch all the crap.

There was a time no matter how much it snowed,

If you needed milk or sugar, it could be bought.

All the shops were open for business, nothing closed

Hoof marks, footprints, and wagon tracks were everywhere in the snow.

There was a time when the winter snow was a
beautiful sight.

Nobody stayed home because of snow.

They went out dining and dancing,

Joyfully celebrating under lantern light.

There was a time when snow remained white all
winter long.

What we see today is paved and cinder-plowed streets

Filthy black-topped snow, which lasts until late spring,

When it is finally gone.

There was a time when no foreboding forecasts
cautioned us to stay home.

The closest neighbor is where you borrowed a cup of
sugar.

And you paid it back when you got your next order
from your grocer.

In those days, in many ways, life was simpler.

There was a time when men were men, ladies were
ladies, and friends were friends--forever.

And the church, school, and shop doors closed--almost
never.

Broken Wings

Alone on a leafless oak tree branch was perched a young sparrow,

Having a mother but no father was to her constant sorrow.

Endowed with colorful plumage, she was ready to fly,

But no matter how hard she tried, she couldn't but didn't know why.

Even though born with a damaged wing, she desperately wanted to try.

"Why, Mother? Why am I so broken and unlike other birds can't fly?"

"Oh, dear sparrow daughter, like an angel you could sing.

Try to remember that flying isn't everything."

Her every attempt failed, and it saddened her more so when others flew.

The time to leave passed, and her momma bird did, too.

Alone with the thought she couldn't get off the ground because of a broken wing.

In her pure heart, if daddy bird could be found, proudly her heart would sing.

Alone in her nest, her tiny, feathered heart kept a rhythmic beat,

Searching all the trees in the forest, checking each other nest,

In the hope that with a father bird,

She would finally pass the test.

"If he soars like an eagle or has a broken wing like me,

If he loves me, I'll be happy,

And with love, maybe we can both be healed

To fly away from the branch of this oak tree."

As the morning sun warmed the September air, she made one last attempt,

Hoping maybe he'll be there.

Her takeoff was okay, until she rapidly fell and landed on a park bench.

There sat her father sparrow, with thinning plumage and the rest snowy white.

All the swallow's instincts had been proven to be right.

There Was a Time

There was a time you'd get chicken for a dime.

Down the street you'd go to the butcher you know.

Five cents a pound for ground round.

He knew everyone by name,

And treated them all the same.

There was a time when you'd pay cents for bread.

People all worked hard just to get ahead.

When a poor man was caught without chicken in his pot.

The winters were so cold and summers were so hot.

There was a time men were so proud, when cursing wasn't allowed.

If you had a job, you didn't steal or rob.

Things were cheap, a nickel for ground meat.

Money, I am told, was all backed by gold.

There was a time when drinking too much whiskey wasn't a crime.

And a penny you gladly paid was a penny at the arcade.

When asking a girl to dance, wasn't taking a chance

When five bucks was a fin you were gin
And loose as a goose at the kissing booth.

There was a time when gasoline was five gallons for a
buck.
You drove for weeks in your eight-cylinder car or
truck.

Those were the days in our glorious land,
When instead of fist-bumping, people shook your
hand.

There was a time when a dollar was a dollar and a
dime was a dime,
And people made out just fine.

Rapid Cycling

Down, down, down, so far down
So far down, so near the bottom
Close to the ground
Where peace can't be found.

High, high, high, up so high
A soul on fire, burning with fever and desire
In love with the sun and the sky.

Down, down, down, in a self-burning hell
So far down, in and out of a dark spell
No one to listen, no one to tell.

Up, up, up, so high up,
Everything is beautiful; I want to live in my high,
To never again cry.

Tomorrow is here, and I'm going down, down, down
Closer to the bottom; closer to the ground
Where peace can't be found.

From a dark sleep, my eyes are open, and I'm high, so
high.
Higher than all of the planets in the sky,
A place that I'm not afraid to go and die.

Down, down, down, so far down
So far down, farther down, digging below the ground
Searching for pills that can't be found.

High, high, high, higher than the sky
The family so near, so near I can see my mother's eye
So high, so high, it's an okay day to die.

Down, down, down, so far down
So far down I'm into the ground
Where my peace is found.

Dark Side

Residing in my distant, dark soul
Are secret lies masquerading as innocent truths
And well hidden sins deep in a black, murky hole
So shamefully committed in my youth.

Secrets so entrenched they can never be told
So soul-damaging a darkness
That will never be bleached by the sun
On cold ominous rainy days, they beg me to confess.

If revealed, would end all the good I've ever done.
Attempts to dismiss those secrets deep down inside
As a way of life other children have to hide
Are quickly set aside as more self-loathing alibis.

Happy, feel-good songs bring tears to my tired eyes.
I know these secrets must go with me to the grave.
Where forever buried will find rest for my secret lies--
An old man's secrets, himself he never forgave.

A truth sadder than all those secrets and lies

Is a life lived as a good man cloaked in secret
deception

Among decent people under clear skies

Without suspicion.

A black-feathered friend once landed on me and
seemed to say,

"You'll be forgiven as you enter Alpha Centauri

On your final day."

As he flew away, he said, "I'm an old crow, and my
eyes are like yours, blurry!"

Fresh Fruit

It's a cloudy day with peeks of sunshine winking at
me.

Sitting on a branch, high up in an apple tree

Is the most evil-looking man staring at me,

Laughing in a menacing way. Is it the devil I see?

Shaking and laughing, every apple falls to the ground.

Apples ripe, fresh, red, and perfectly round

Land safely on green grass, waiting to be found.

The devil, still laughing, shrieks, "To me, you're
bound!"

Time passed all those once fresh, beautiful apples by,

While the devil grunts and groans, joyfully watching
them die.

Their once young, ripe, red skin, which pleased the
eye,

Was never enjoyed by anyone, now rots under the sky.

Having destroyed every apple, he was now leaving
behind,

Laughing along the way, certain another apple he'd
find.

In the holler, he was heard shrieking, "I hope you don't mind.

I'm here to make sure all the fruit of this tree is mine!"

An angry farmer cursed, waving his finger to the devil in the tree,

"Look at all these rotten apples. How could you do this to me?"

Mockingly, the devil imputes, "You're the only ass I see!

You should gather fruit as it falls fresh from the tree!"

Echoes

Willing fingers desperate to write
Caress a keyboard with anger and quiet rage.
Empty as a black, starless night
Are the disparate fingers on a blank page.

A world where every word has been spoken,
No lyrics are left for new songs to be sung.
Artists add their easels to the piles already broken
As the abject fingers are wrung.

Fearing the hopeless replaying in his head
Will explode into fragments of hatred
And self-loathing vile until he is dead.
Relaxing fingers conclude nothing is sacred.

His fingers off the keyboard end his rage.
The dark night sky clears, and the moon glows.
It's okay to be an empty page.
Just listen to the echoes.

To agree that all has been written
And all has been sung or spoken

Is as false as snowshoes on a kitten
Or an artist's last brushstroke.

When a newborn baby's eyes are first opened,
Everything in the world is new again.
Listen to the echoes; the crow has spoken.
Now count to 10.

A Slice of Heaven

A well-dressed woman with a pained look on her face,

Twirling a string of pearls sparkled her affluence with the diamonds on her finger.

Approached a diapered guru sitting in a lotus position occupying his personal space.

With hesitancy in her trembling voice, she said, "There's this, well, you see I'm a singer."

"Madam, please sit, relax, tell me what it is that's troubling you."

"I'm wealthy as you can no doubt see, and I have all the money I need to see me through.

I need to know if you can tell me where is God's heaven?"

"My dear young lady, where have you been looking?

Have you been looking above and beyond the stars seeking a confession?

Or is it the comfort of all your worldly goods as a paradise you have mistaken?"

"I've been a kind, decent person to all my servants and staff.

I followed the golden rule as best I could.

I sang in the choir during every Sunday mass

A Heart Searching for Its Soul

I donated food and clothing to my old neighborhood.

So, everything I did and places I've been, there's this
Fear of the hereafter I believe I misunderstood."
The trembling voice devolved into sobs as she sat with
Her elbows on her knees and both hands to her chin.

The lotus-sitting guru, undaunted, asked, "Where
shall we begin?
In spite of all that you did and the places you've been
In your heart and soul there's this avarice you have
deeply hidden.

None of any of this matters, nothing under the
morning sun.
Nor the night stars and moon's glow.
No confession will cleanse what you have done.
There is no hereafter, all there is, is only the here and
now.

During your quest for wealth and fame, that's all been
fun.
Yet no peace of mind have you found.
Now you ask me where is heaven?

From your birth throughout all your days on Earth,

Every place you sang and all the flowers you held in your diamond-fingered hands,

Every single step you ever took on the firmament of this precious land,

Have no doubt or regrets: It's the only heaven or hell any of us will ever get.

Madam, where you and I now sit is our slice of God's heaven.

Learn, as I have, to love it."

Coming Soon—Maybe

There may be a day when the wind will be still,
And the trees will wonder why.
The whippoorwills no longer cry.
When the racoon caught in the moonlight
Will be confused by the silence of the night.

A time may come when enemies
Will no longer fight wars, each with a gun.
That's when evil madmen will launch weapons
So powerful that they block the Earth's sun.

Because white men, thinking they're the chosen one,
Are burdened by demagogues whose hunger for
power is extreme.
It will result in a time when trees, birds, racoons, and
all life on Earth will be wiped clean.
That's the day when the wind will be still.

The Shallow Part of a Raging River

Like yesterday and all the days before, I awoke to an old familiar song,

A song without lyrics, which was 84 years long.

With the morning optimism joining my early morning walk,

I happened upon an old, wise man, who was sitting on a rock.

"Excuse me, old sir, do you have a moment to talk?"

"Why, of course, I do. Come sit by my side!"

"Well, sir, I have this problem bothering me, and I'm trying to decide

If those around me know there's something I'm trying to hide."

"Go on!"

"I suppose I should begin by saying I have this recurring shame,

And is it me who's the ultimate blame?"

"Go on!"

"It's amazing here I am confessing what I don't
understand to you

A man sitting on a rock.

Are you listening to me?

Or are you just letting me talk?"

"You were saying something about a problem and
shame and is it yourself to blame.

Well, I'm listening, but there's a hesitancy in your
voice.

Trust me, or not.

For now, it's your choice."

"Well, I do."
"Then please go on."

"I want to ask you what it is about singing without
lyrics in a song.

What does it mean?"

"It means that you're using me to tell you what it
means."

"I'm sorry if that's what you believe.

I'll be here tomorrow on this same rock,

If you're out for a morning walk and wish to talk.

Let's start from the beginning when you were a child."

"Okay, old sir," I said, as I walked away with a crying smile.

Soon it was another morning with a cloudy sky and rain on the way.

It was a good night's sleep with a dream giving me more to say.

I hurried to the rock, eager more than ever to share.

But neither the man nor the rock was there!

Like yesterday and all the days before, I awoke to an old, familiar song,

A song without lyrics, which was 84 years long.

There never was an old man on a rock; it always was me with myself, suppressing the secrets of all my wrongs.

My well-hidden secrets that remain deep inside

Repeat the lyrics, "I tried! I tried! I tried!"

Are You Eating Poisonous Mushrooms?

Putins, Hitlers, and Mussolinis are popping up

Throughout America like mushrooms after an April rain.

Holier than thou are the Christians from Arizona to the coastal shores of Maine.

Swastikas are proudly being worn on the left shirt sleeve.

While the American emblem is worn on the right.

Arrogantly, they parade through our cities and towns

Like thugs and thieves in the night.

In their rank, no black, red, or yellow skins are visible. They're all white.

A Man Called Jesus

Two thousand and twenty-one years ago on this
planet Earth

Walked a dark-haired bearded man who preached

Followed by believers who joined in his search.

They all died sans the truth they never reached.

His name was Jesus, a simple man and nothing more.

He was a carpenter when lumber was rare.

And there, too, was Peter, who fished from the shore.

They talked of a God in the warm sun's glare.

And then there was John, whose mother was
Elizabeth.

She spoke often with her cousin Mary

About their two sons and the spreading holy spirit
myth.

The rumors that flew from the people were often
scary.

"It's a process," said some other damn fool.

"Simple to explain, Jesus, just changed his name!"

It's a sign then of how fast time flew.

There was a story about Gabriel going around

An angel with a horn, who lured the holy spirit to
town.

Patiently waiting was Mary, and a match was found.
His horn, still blowing, was heard loud and clear all
around.
And Elizabeth, not wanting to be outdone
With a baron husband, Zachariah, found a way
For the holy spirit to give them a son.
And John the Baptist was born to help us all pray.

So, there they were, Mary and Elizabeth, the mothers.
Whose mysterious pregnancies caused much
discourse.
About Jesus and john, the two spirited brothers,
Who roamed and preached of a God who created our
Earth.

And as it became a creed, not wishing to displease
The rumors eventually did subside.
And people throughout all the land fell on their knees
Looking for more miracles from God, they cried.

And so it would come to pass the Jesuses, Johns, and Judases

All gave up their beards, sandals, and robes.

As the years became centuries, and weeds turned to grass,

The good men now all wear fancy-tailored clothes.

As in the story being told, God made man in his own image.

And in the year 2015 on an escalator ride,

Preaching to the cheering crowd about their souls he alone could save

He had no beard, sandals, nor robes on his downward stride.

As were all the self-made Gods before who lived and died.

Every village and town had temple steeples built higher than the sky.

There were always more Peters and Judases lurking by,

Waiting to betray their masters, not caring nor knowing why.

So life with all its people somehow always seem to
survive

Somehow there is always a God to replace the Gods
before him

And innocent hopeful prayerful people buying all the
lies.

Faithfully believing he will forgive all their sins.

What a wonderful world it would be if all our fathers
were deities.

To walk on water and part the seas,

Instead of killing and dividing you and me.

Gabriel, put your rusty horn away,

Spirits aren't getting girls pregnant today!

Possession

Alone I stood in the sun, proclaiming I am one

The only one, except for that shadow following me.

Whispers from dark clouds forming in the sky

Told me the shadow soon would be free.

And so would I.

With one foot on solid land and the other in the desert sand,

One hand had several stones, and the other was full of slippery sand.

Both hands held tightly to the stones and sand until the grips were so painfully tight.

As the palms released the stones and the sand from the possessive hand, he understood freeing them was right.

How easily the sand poured through my fingers back to the waiting sand.

While three stones still in the other I paused to realize their art, their soul and beauty, so much to understand.

Frozen, unable to turn away, knowing it was time to go,

Nothing is forever, except forever, is this vexing thought telling me I must let things go.

When an echo from ominous clouds above said,

"Get both feet back on solid ground

And your freedom will be found

As you move ahead."

Things Change

My heart is suspicious, like a cat peeking out from behind an evergreen tree.

Will my soul trust what's out there, waiting for me?

Maybe if I stick my head out a little further, a little bit at a time,

I'll be able to see if there's any danger, or maybe the humans will be old friends of mine.

If I allow my instincts to go full-out from behind this tree and be in open view,

Will my soul wave me back into hiding, signaling the humans aren't the ones I once knew.

Time Flies

I awoke to a sunny day, thinking, "It's almost July

My, oh my, how quickly time passes by!"

A flock of geese show off their colors and please the
eye.

I take a deep breath and thank God I'm still alive.

Soon we'll celebrate the Fourth.

Streets with flags draped from every porch

Will capture the spirits of veterans parading by.

It's almost July. How quickly time passes by.

Take a deep breath and blink your eyes.

Listen and hear throughout the land,

While children and some may never understand

The Founding Fathers and the sacrifices they gave.

And the millions of patriots in their grave.

The parades will soon be over, and the jets will retreat
from the skies.

Empty cemeteries will hear some of the last cries.

Every red, white, and blue symbol retires to the parks
and grills outside.

Gray-haired patriots don their aprons, getting ready for their hot dogs to fry.

And all the laughing, fat bellies force another beer and cry.

The day is almost over; there's an ominous darkening, dark red sky.

Broken by sparklers and fireworks exploding high.

The babies are yawning; it's time for their nightly lullaby.

Reality breaks the spell as I wipe dry my eyes.

Morning after has the smell of beer cans and leftover French fries.

Three Tylenols later, your headache recalls the reason why.

You were a civilian patriot, sending rockets into the July sky.

Now the eerie silence pervades the empty sighs.

It's almost next July and time to say our goodbyes!

The River

I took an early morning stroll
Down by the riverside to watch the water flow.
Something my weary morning eyes couldn't hide
Was my emotional pride.

There was a path along the way
Whereas a child I used to play.
But that was a long time ago,
Steadily gazing at the river, it seemed to slow.

Memories of a better time come and go.
As the water would speed and then slow.
So much has happened since the radio:
Summers are shorter, and winters have less snow.

The river on its journey hurries over the rocks and
floating debris.
At times grabbing an overhanging tree.
Like a magnet, its force wants to carry me.
I muse, "If I let go, will I at last be free?"

The early morning stroll to the river's edge

As poignant was it was, was as empty as my walk
back to the cottage.

With the sound of rushing water replaying in my head

And the rest of the day still stretching out ahead.

With a vengeance like the rushing waters, the hours
fled

To a sunset of deep purple and crimson red.

Where upon a horizon my soul will dance silhouettes

Freely until the evening ends all standing bets.

I'll take an early evening stroll to the river's banks,

Listening to the rushing water flow,

Pretending I'm on my knees to give thanks

For all the wonders in the universe mankind will
never know.

I am the river; I am the stars and the moon.

Imagineering it all, but tonight I'll be alone in my
room.

I'll sleep through the night, while the river continues
to flow,

Searching for answers, I realize nothing is what it
seems,

Except for the dreamer's dreams.

Turning

Some leaves are turning and already beginning to fall.
In the farmer's field, corn stalks are nearly four feet tall.
In a nearby hospital, you can hear an infant's first cry.
In a nursing home, I hear an old lady's last sigh.

"There's always tomorrow," some will say.
But that's all well and good for the young here today.
Echoes from a passing dark cloud relates
Something about love and hate that can't be faked.
More often, fools of both it does make.

The echoes loudly intensify the baby's first cry.
And also it heightens the old lady's last sigh.
As heard by an artist while he paints his last stroke
Of a falling leaf beneath a large oak.

Throughout the day and into the evening sky
A passerby heard an old lady's last sigh,
While a sailor watched his day at sea die,
Whispering to the moon, "I'm still alive."

The cries and the sighs of the day were all gone.
So peacefully, so beautifully, so calm.

A Boy in the Rain

I swung out of bed, still groggy-eyed, when I peered through my windowpane.

Blinking my sleepy eyes and to my surprise, was I dreaming again?

Was this a trick or some sort of mind game?

The street was sunny on one side while on the other was wet with rain.

Sitting on the street getting wet was a boy who didn't seem to mind.

While above him a bird was crowing on a telephone line.

"Where, dear God, was his father or mother?"

I was shouting louder and louder, but my voice was silent.

The louder I shouted, the quieter my voice seemed to be.

My panicked voice didn't matter; it didn't make a dent.

What ever is the matter with me?

My voiceless voice entered into the astral plane.

Nothing seemed to matter; the boy still sat in the rain.

Again, I shouted, "Get out of the rain!

I promise to never bother you again!"

Suddenly, the boy turned his head, looked at me, and shouted,

"I heard every damn word you said!"

With both of my hands,

I held onto my troubled head.

Then the alarm clock went off,

And I realized that I was still in bed.

In a Word

While walking one day in the shopping mall,

I ran into an old friend of mine.

He stopped short in his greetings and said, "There's a word I'd like you to define.

It's been bugging me for quite some time."

"Well, old pal, give me the word, and I'll help you if I can."

"Integrity."

"That's easy yet difficult. It's all about the quality

For example, Elizabeth Cheney."

"I don't get it," he said.

"Allow me to explain. It's about honesty and principle, you see.

She defied her own party to fight for the truth and democracy.

That, my friend, is integrity."

September

It was the morning of August 31.

I opened the door and smelled the September sun.

As exhilarating as the moment was,

Another month of my life was done.

Like a patchwork quilt, the sun shines in spots through the forest trees.

Acorns lie in waiting among the fallen leaves.

Bluish red brown is the color of September as seen by cornstalks turning brown.

I wonder, "How many more Septembers will come around?"

I stood and stared for a moment longer to take the September scent in.

It all passed as I let the hungry cat come in,

And feeling sheepish, let out a grin.

It was August 31,

When I smelled the September sun.

Empty Bucket

The storm is over, and the parade has passed.

All the passion is gone.

The bucket is empty, and the majorettes

Have all twirled their last baton.

Desperate to be relevant in a world swiftly passing by,

Listening to a marching band from inside a closed door

Like an empty bucket outside in the pouring rain

When passed is still dry.

The sound of drums fades into the distance, and the parade is gone forevermore

No matter how hard you try or how silent is your cry,

The bucket remains dry.

Yet the scent of lilies won't close the last door.

Mood Swings

When the night gives way to the waiting dawn,
And your heart wakes to yesterday's song,
You humbly ask, "Was my every song sung
Or every word written, right or wrong?"

Can you hear me? Do you hear me, spiritual higher
power somewhere in the heavenly sky?
My secular soul prays you will make all the ones I love
Special angels when I say goodbye.

The accent lights are still beautifying the quiet night
Whispering, "The last party was just right."

The Last Party

One act, one show, one life, one chance for success
Or abject loneliness.
All the time from the cradle to the grave
Is all you ever had and all you ever gave.

The celebrations are over; the balloons all said "bye."
They rose one by one, popping in the crimson sky.
The violins and horns are all back in their cage.
As the musicians and singers have all left the stage.

Alone, unable to complete your lonely feelings,
You replay memories of sickness, then healing.
Colored accent lights soften the moonless night.
Your inner Italianesque is tacking to the right.

In your quiet solitude, you ponder all the reasons,
Reliving the sorrows and joys of past seasons.
Closing your eyes, you follow a narrow bright path,
Which slowly dims, until it becomes dark as the sky.
And there we are, just you and I,
Two tears, destined to never dry.

Our Soul Was Found

Sasha, our Argentian Dogo, has earned our family's love. Years ago, she saved my wife's life when she became ill. As you can see in the photo, she's now in the driver's seat! No more evidence of our soul is needed.

The End!

About the Author

I am a high school dropout who completed his GED while serving in the US Army. At that time, I also completed training at the Military Police Academy and worked as a confinement specialist while stationed overseas. The Army gave me the opportunity to further my education, and I was able to take classes at the University of Maryland.

In later years, I was provided the opportunity to attend a two-year program at Hazleton General Hospital to be certified as a Supportive Physical Therapist. This was followed by completion of a certificate program for Personnel Management earned at King's College, in Wilkes-Barre, Pennsylvania, and the completion of training at the Pennsylvania Department of Corrections Academy.

My employment history has been varied. I worked in heavy industry, marketing, and as a corrections officer in a state prison. I also owned my own business, a neighborhood tavern. My personal highest satisfaction was while working in a variety of capacities, with the elderly, disabled children, and men and women with developmental disabilities.

I believe in community service, and I served on the boards of my local American Heart Association and Arthritis Foundation. I was also interested in the arts and physical fitness, and I was a member of the Board of Governors of the local Art League, and I founded the Hazleton Jogging Club, where I had lived.

My community involvement also included my membership in the local VFW Chapter 8225 and served in various capacities, including Commander. I was elected Mayor of the Borough of Beaver Meadows, and I served in that position for 12 years, having been elected for three terms.

My personal accomplishments include authoring several books: *Final Duty*, the updated edition *Fallow's Final Duty, Bits & Pieces of an Ordinary Man's Life*, and finally *A Heart Searching for Its Soul*.

CPSIA information can be obtained
at www.ICGtesting.com
Printed in the USA
BVHW060050051122
651121BV00004B/46